Are you a Spider?

For Tom M.-J.A.

SRAonline.com

Printed in the U.S.A.

Send all inquiries to:
SRA/McGraw-Hill
4400 Easton Commons
Columbus, OH 43219-6188

ISBN 978-0-07-612265-3
MHID 0-07-612265-4

10 11 12 LHN 22 21

The McGraw-Hill Companies

Are you a Spider?

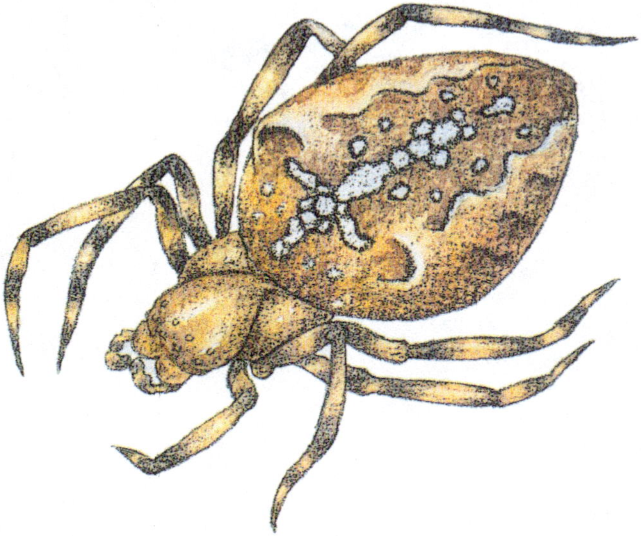

Judy Allen and Tudor Humphries

McGraw Hill SRA

Columbus, OH

Are you a spider?
If you are, your mother
looks like this, and
spins webs.

Your mother laid eggs
and wrapped them in
a special silk pouch.
You are inside of one of them.

When you break out of your egg,
you will find you have a lot
of brothers and sisters.

You are all small,
but you will all get **bigger.**

You look perfect.

You have a tiny waist and eight hairy legs.

You have two handy claws for pushing food into your mouth.

You have eight eyes.

You have six spinnerets hidden under your body. They are for spinning silk thread.

Silk thread is the most important thing in your life.

Begin to spin some at once.

You need it to help you move away and start your new life.

Spin out the thread so it floats in the air. With luck, a breeze will catch it and carry you away.

Or you could just walk.

Use your silk thread as a safety line when you walk.

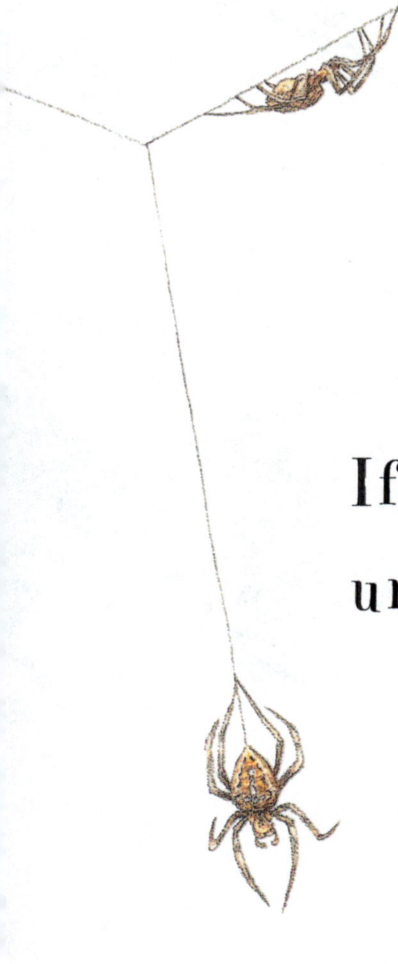

If you fall, hang from your line until you stop swinging.

Then climb back up it again.

Use your silk thread to build a web.

A web will catch flies,
and flies are good to eat.

Attach these threads first.
These threads must be
very strong.

This is hard work.

Attach these
threads next.

These threads
must be very sticky.

This is even
harder work.

Congratulations!
You have built a beautiful web.

When a fly flies
into your web, it will
stick there. Run and bite it.

Your bite will make
it go to sleep.

You can eat it now.

Or you can wrap it in silk thread and save it for later.

Watch out for birds.
Birds are dangerous.
Birds eat spiders.

Hide under a leaf.
That way the birds
won't see you.

Keep one foot on your web. If the web shakes, you will know you have caught a fly.

Watch out for wasps.
Wasps are dangerous.
A wasp sting can
kill a spider.

If you catch a
wasp in your web,
don't try to eat it.
Try to cut it free.

Be sure to keep away from
the end that stings.

However, if you look something like this

or this

or this

or this

you are not a spider.

You are . . .

. . . a human child.

You do not have
eight eyes or
eight hairy legs.

You might have a
tiny waist, but you
definitely don't have
spinnerets, and you
can't spin silk thread.

But you can do a lot of things
that spiders can't do.

You must still be careful of wasps,
but you don't have to bother
making a web.

Best of all, you will never, ever, EVER have to wrap up a fly and eat it.

Did You Know . . .

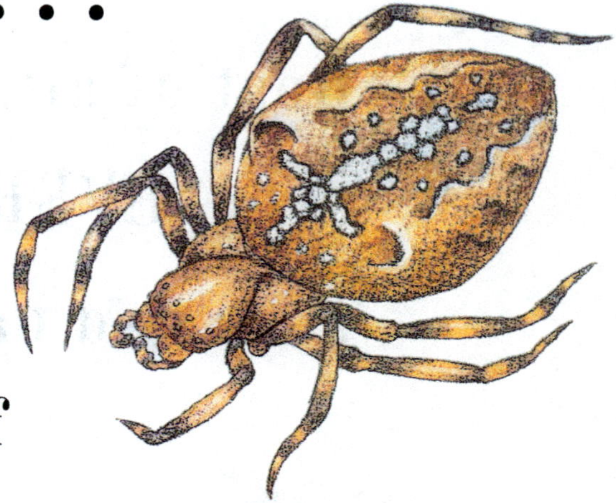

. . . spider silk is very strong and elastic, and spinning it takes a lot of energy. When a web is damaged, a spider will often eat it before making a new one.

. . .there are more than 35,000 different kinds of spiders in the world.

. . . this is a garden spider, but other kinds include jumping spiders, trap-door spiders, water spiders, crab spiders, tarantulas, wandering spiders, spitting spiders, and tropical orb-web spiders, whose webs are more than six feet wide.

. . . the goliath tarantula has a legspan almost as wide as a dinner plate.